what i meant to say

what i meant to say

Julia Burr

poems

Copyright © 2026 Julia Burr

All rights reserved. No part of this book may be reproduced, stored or transmitted in any form or by any means without prior written permission from the author, except for brief quotations in reviews.

First published in 2026.

ISBN: 978-1-7644626-0-0

Typeset and Cover Design by Julia Burr
Photograph by Julia Burr

If you have any feedback you would like to share or want to reach out to the author, please email: julia.burr@hotmail.com

part 1: being me

or the overwhelming and multi-faceted experience of being an individual

1

part 2: you and i

or the confusing complexity we encounter in relating with others

41

part 3: being in this world

or the union of beauty and pain that lies in the experience of being an individual in the complexity of this world

69

part 1: being me

or the overwhelming and multi-faceted experience of being an individual

Behind the Silence

Sometimes I stay silent
because even if I tried to explain,
you could never understand
the Bigness of what l feel.

No words or sounds could represent
the abyss of my experience.
The most vibrant colours couldn't sing
the song of my expansion.
No fabric, taste or smell could tell
the story of this moment.

Even if I put it all
into a museum,
an immersive experience showering you
in the gooey acid of truth,
you would only ever get a grasp
the size of a yellow sand grain.
Would you attempt to comprehend
all parts of the universe?

I am the mind of a million stars
burning, flying, falling, dying.
I am a body of thunder and lightning,
electric shocks of pleasure and pain
united in each breath.

I am as many different emotions
as there are water drops in the ocean.

I am too big to fit
into the secret shrine
space of your heart.
And yet all I need is the feeling
of folding into your arms.

May you take this as request
in moments I stay silent,
to cradle me into your chest
So that my self won't fall apart
like a house of cards
in the face of the intensity
of forever being me.

How are you?

Maybe I'm amnesic
or maybe I'm aphasic?
Somehow, I can't find the words
to paint the untamed turmoil
that rages inside my mind.
I'm a multi-storey house
held up by emotional walls
ready to collapse, implode,
detonate. Personalities splitting
into crises dissociating
into fragments of vanished
identities.
Who is I and where?
Are you?
I am trembling like aspen
in a vinegar-soaked breeze
praying for peace.

Like trees, leaves, birds
and dragonflies
I want to be a poem
written by the earth.

I watch my anxiety
on a Ferris wheel ride
joyfully juggling

my rolling thoughts.
A shed full of chickens
and the fox got in.
I haven't only met my wolf,
I run with it like women do.

So, how do I tell you
what I'm feeling today
if I can't even see
the surface anymore?
I pause, breathe, swallow and type:

I'm well. How are you?

Archive of Hopes

My heart is a museum of everyone I've ever loved.
Memories got locked away behind bulletproof glass,
Collecting dust from the erosion
of tears, fears, and heavy emotion,
the ashes of love once burning,
the ground-down passion once yearning.
And next to each exhibit
there's a rock-shaped piece of my heart.
I had carved them out myself one day
with the fatal blade of trust.

I gave and gave and gave my soul
and only got breadcrumbs back.

Empty-handed and broken-hearted,
I stare at the fragments of me:
Solid heart shards,
Motionless
No beat, no rhythm,
No will left to dance,
Starved by their hunger for romance.
Cabinets lining the wall of my heart
display the shatters like pieces of art.

With every new collectable
I want to burn it down.

I want to cease the dreadful game
and stop the endless pain.

And yet, I will keep chipping away
because I'm addicted to hope.

Who am I?

I am a migrant
and I am privileged as fuck
Compared to other people
my best friend has always been luck.
I am white girl
who moved to the country
of the first First Nation people
Always is and always will be
The oldest human culture on Earth
a land taken and colonised
by white Europeans
who forgot to pack respect in their bags
when they set out to settle
where they didn't belong.

Have I set out to follow them?
Am I one of the bad guys?

I am German.
People hear my accent,
call me Nazi
and I am breaking
being taken
to the ground of shame
for my nationality, a part of my identity,
because I hate my nation's legacy.

My passport is dark red
the colour of dried blood.
Why does its cover show an eagle
if my wings are clipped?
I tried to fly so far away
I never broke free
Got stuck feeling broken
Ancient guilt is glued to my roots
like chewing gum to the sole of my shoes
weighing me down
I want to drown
in morning dew.
I want to fall
into an endless black hole,
be sucked in
become one with the void.
But I will not avoid
my duty.

I am not my nation's past,
not even my own.
I have a choice
and I choose to use my voice
to speak words of truth and love.
I choose to march for freedom and peace.
I choose to protect trees, birds and the bees.
I will send you photographs of daisies,

but I will never rip them out.

I cannot let the history books
tell me I'm not good enough
to bring my good into the world.

My grandma was a beacon of joy.
She taught me how to multiply
the sunshine that I carried within.
Now all that German love won't fit
into the little space between my ribs.

Unstoppable Train

I'm lying in bed
the thoughts in my head
sit heavy on my chest
like a weighted blanket

I am craving rest
but instead I run
like a hamster in a wheel
Tap tap tap
The wheel squeaks, screams, cries out
The sound of my anxiety
wraps its greedy claws
around my heart, my lung, my throat
and I
        can't
                b r e a t h e

I close my eyes,
I clench my fingers,
holding onto the sheets
as if they were my rescue boat
in a wild and stormy sea
The waves of the night
wash over me
rumbling and tumbling

An ocean of emotion
swallowing me
drowning me
Invisible hands are gripping my neck
choking me
suffocating me
as the noise in my head
gets louder and wilder
rolling like thunder
blaring chaos
erupting
exploding
imploding

Until I reach
my hand from below the covers
up high to grasp
the light of stars
in the darkest night.

A moment of silence
A moment of hope.

But the thought train won't stop
It ratters and tatters
throughout the whole night
tnd the rushing pace

causes delays
on the endless journey
to a destination
called peace.

Will I ever get there?

Breaking Through the Blue

I dive through waves
into unknown depths of silence
to find ripples of light
breaking through the blue
dancing at the bottom of the ocean
that is me.

A Day at the Workshop

I still remember the day
my dad took me to work with him
He used to run a well known
painting business in town.
I climbed a scaffold by his side
Three metres up, the outlook vast
A pirate on a vessel's mast
I painted wooden slats like swords
between big tubs and cans of paint
Hidden corners, angles, ladders
A young explorer's treasured world
Rainbow drizzles and colourful blops
across the workshop walls
like fairy footprints everywhere
making the concrete floor smirk.
It was one of my favourite days.
The smell of paint still makes me smile.

Every Woman

Sometimes I see myself in the mirror
and I want my old eating disorder back,
the one that was bequeathed to me
by my anorexic mother
when I was 15 years old
and trying to figure out
what I had to do
to be loved
to feel
as if someone could eventually love me.

Now I confuse the chase for dopamine
that resides in chocolate pudding
with soothing self-love.
I am nauseous from the bullshit
that life made me swallow.

The Essence of Life

My mum taught me joy
when she took me to the park
to feed ducks and swans
on the autumn-coloured lawn
I always shared a bite with them
At home, she made hot chocolate,
topped it with whipped cream
she added chocolate shavings
a little girl's dream

My mother taught my bliss
I remember a photograph of her
She ued to have curly, brown hair
Her neck tilted back,
blowing bubbles in the air,
reflections of the sunset
in iridescent spheres,
a warm golden flair
There was an expression on her face
It was soft, it was bliss,
it was feminine grace
She looked just like the evening sun,
peaceful and fun
A picture of the essence of life.

The One

You are the one who always knew
how to hold me safe
You're the one who always saw
my softness as my gift
You're the one who always held
my hand when I lost sight
You're the one who I could trust
when the world seemed cold and dark

It was your love that made me strong
It was your faith that kept me going
It was your drive that let me grow
It was your voice that taught me forgiveness

I am who I am today
because you never left
I am still becoming more
because I adore you
I have found my magic
in my tenderness
I have grown the courage
to be seen as who I am

Because I am you
and you have always been me
Because you always loved me.

The Monthly Anguish

If I write this poem
a miracle has happened
My brain feels numb
My mind is blocked
Anxiety is crippling me
I wish I could just let it flow
Feel light, find words
filled with caramel toffee fudge
gooey beauty inside
Sweetness on the tip of your tongue
a soothing sound when you speak it out loud
melting the numbness away
Instead, melted chocolate
has stained my woollen blanket
A rather joyful mess
I wish I could sigh
and say in bliss
"Well, that was worth it, wasn't it?"
And dopamine would flow again
through crimson jellied veins
But instead here I lie
brain fogged and nauseous
My chest feels deflated
I want to be able to breathe again
I can't bear the monthly bleed's pain.

Between Her and Me

I look into her eyes
and I only see beauty.
Warm glowing amber
uniting her fierceness with kind gentleness.
I watch her body flow
as she dances through the room,
creating new shapes,
rearranging her shadows -
A mesmerizing play
of light and dark,
owning her space
- an energetic field of awe.

I adore all of her,
every little inch.
I only feel love
admiring her grace.

I look into the mirror,
into my own blue eyes.
They shine, but it isn't the sparkling of joy.
It is the silky glimmer of tears of despair.

Tears filled with pain, infused with shame.

Shame for myself, my body, my softness.
Tears filled with pain, infused with blame.
I blame myself for not being better.
Staring at myself, -------------- her, -------------- that body
as if it was an object of true disgust.

And it hurts so much what I do to myself.
I want to scream and shout and yell it all out -

Please stop!

I don't understand.

Why can't I stop?
Even though I know better.
My heart knows better.
And it starts to stand up and fight my brain.
'You wouldn't do this to anyone else.
Neither Freund, nor Feind, friend or foe.'
My heart fights without armour
- a warrior of love -
And for the first time, it finally says, 'No.'

When my mind is at war,
losing hope in the battle,
When compliments are turned
and twisted, distorted,

My heart whispers, 'Stop.'
'Remember the truth.'
I grant you permission
to own your beauty.
I grant you permission
to dance and receive
words from the hearts
of others, who love.

Because life is beautiful
on every single day.
My existence is beautiful
and so am I.

Ode to My Body

Eyes like the sky
Airy blue with the softness
of rain laden clouds.
The sparkling of a million stars
mirrored in tears of joy,
filled with love stories.

Your smile
strips them off their armour,
pierces through defensive walls,
pulls on the rubber bands
of pretending masks.
They have no chance.

Your shoulders are strong
from carrying
the weight of the good girl
of perfection and elegance.
Like mountains carry
the weight of the sky.

The ripeness
of your breasts
deserves to be worn
with pride.

Nature's sweetest fruit
Seducing Venus herself.

The centre piece
is an oasis
of tenderness
and safety.
Your belly is my sacred temple
of holy femininity.

Your hips sing
a song
of empowerment.
They swing
to the rhythm
of fire and ash.

Your legs are a remembrance
of the eternal marriage
between strength and womanhood.
Made so that a young girl could run,
grown strong
for the woman to stand up.

Follow the curved path
up your thighs to find
the well of pleasure.

A luscious lake,
here to water
whatever my lands want to birth.

My Names

'What was your name again?'
If I would only know
The one name I should be.

Once my name was river
When wildness flooded all my veins
When I surrendered to flow.

Once I was called tree
When I grew deep, grounding roots
To hold up against the storm.

Once my name was bird
When I flew to reach new heights
To travel, breathe, be free.

Once I was called mountain
When I learned to carry the weight
Of grief upon my shoulders.

Once I was named fire
When passion burned inside me
And I learned to befriend my anger.

Once my name was sky

Sparkling like a million stars
The universe in my eyes.

Once I was named ocean
When I held my heart wide open
To flood the world with love.

So, what is my name today
As I am everything I've been?
The strong, the soft, the sovereign

Defined by constant change
Call me what you think suits best
Who do you think I am?

Run

The crisp cold
brushes the tip
of my nose before
I open my eyes
The darkness of the
young day
pushes against my window
The morning's icy greetings
have sneaked in through
the cracks of the wooden window
frame to say
Hello.

Get up, get dressed,
brush teeth, brush hair,
shoes on, snack in,
coffee down, warm up
Get out.
One breath
and I feel
free.

I start to run.
Sweat
on
skin.

Lost
in
greens.
Dream
in
blues.
Until safety finds her way
home.

Day 14

Sometimes I stare at a black man and wonder
If he thinks that I am racist
When really all I want is
To walk over and kiss him until
Rationality leaves the country
And foolishness gives standing ovation.
Maybe he thinks my staring is racist,
When ovulation has turned me
Into a hot superficialist.

Goodbye Darling

Goodbye my love.
You have been great
Yet I consider myself
to be greater.
Now you may think,
how arrogant
I sound,
what an audacious thing
to say.
I'm a mouth full,
hard to swallow.
I ask you politely
to go ahead
and eat up.
As what you are honoured to witness
is a woman
who has bathed herself
in the silken milk
of self-worth.
She wears it as her crown,
invisible
yet remarkable.
Her back
is straight,
her head

held high.
Not demanded by pride
but borne with grace.
A woman
who says No.
How dare she does?!
She says No
to fitting in-
to the shoe box
society has gifted her.
She declines,
respectfully,
while she unwraps
her world
of infinite opportunities.

And so, my love,
I thank you
for all the times
I was held small,
belittled,
judged too fast
based on innocent looks,

for all the times
when my kindness
was confused

with weakness,
and a lack of confidence.

For if you hadn't shown me
patriarchy's face,
I had never learned
to vote out,
step out,
step up,
rise up
and raise my voice
for other women,
for myself.

Goodbye
norm-kissing conformance
Goodbye
to accusing abuse
for not loving fully
Goodbye
to anyone not believing in me
to not believing in myself.

Goodbye, my love,
you held me small
But I have outgrown
the little girl's mind.

My collection of rejections
does no longer fit
into the
clean glass cabinet
of convenience.
And so, I embrace
the discomfort
of my freedom.

Addicted

I am addicted to everything
that they are labelling as "bad",
Everything they have marginalised,
demonised and pathologised,
branded with shame,
burnt with blame.

I am addicted to feeling
deep and falling deeper,
to loving without reason
unreasonably fierce
with no fear of treason.

I am addicted to men
who cry
and women
who speak up
when everyone else barely dares to think
thoughts deemed illegal.

I am addicted to claiming
my worth.
The pay rise, the title,
commitment,
- respect.
I know I deserve it.

I am addicted to running
against the herd.
I'm rebelling by resting,
finding purpose in silence
in a world that has glamorised
hustle and toil.
I like to grind
in a different way.

I am holding on-
to pleasure, fun and love
in a society that is ruled by an algorithm,
on a planet that feels like a rubbish pit,
at a time when forests are disappearing,
when children are starving, mothers are crying and dads
are fighting.
Because I have to
if I want to make a difference.

So, dress me in disgrace
and drown me in champagne
Because I am addicted to dancing
where they are trying to silence the music.

Dancing with Eros

Venus has sewn her soul
to the sole of my feet
like a shadow
that can only be seen
in my light.

I walk down the street
and meet her everywhere
She made me wear
my dancing shoes
so, I can waltz with Eros.

I always dance to the humming of bees
enveloping velvet leaves.
I bent down to greet
lavender flowers in purple gowns.
I look up to watch the clouds
passing like travelling troubadours,
telling stories of dragons,
collecting rain drops in their cheeks
like hamsters hoarding treasures.

I listen to rain drops
drumming on rocks
and soon, I can smell petrichor,

a waft in the air
bringing hope after drought.
The aroma of summer rain and soil,
the ethereal fluid,
the blood of Gods.

I see Venus everywhere.
Yet, nothing could ever compare
to what I feel for the man,
who carries the soul of her son.
So, this time, I am taking the chance.
I reach out my hand:
Can I have this dance?

part 2: you and i

or the confusing complexity we encounter in relating with others

Your Existence

Your existence
is my favourite thing in the world.
How come you see me without looking?
While everyone else spits out their opinions
with closed eyes, ears and hearts.
They judge me like a picture book[1]
and I swallow the bitter pill of anger.
It gets trapped inside my throat,
eradicates my appetite.
Someone tightened the pressure valve.
Now I'm a volcano, eager to erupt.

Then your message pops up
and I cool down in the blaze.
Your words weave flowers into my hair
reminding me how it feels to be safe.
I don't need to staple fake smiles on my face
I don't need to hide the turmoil inside.

You listen with your heart, soul, mind and presence,
embrace me without touch.
You're in every whispered kiss of the wind,
a bearer of solace and ease.
Your existence is indeed my favourite thing,
A paramount part of my life far away.

---

[1] Line taken from Lana Del Rey's song Brooklyn Baby

The Shape of Your Absence

What is present is the absence of you.
I can feel it, hear it, smell it, see it.
A hole in the centre of my world, dark and empty
Like a gaping maw with teeth like claws
grasping at anything that has colour.

I know your absence is not my fault.
And yet, it feels like abandonment.
How can something that isn't here
hurt deeper than anything I've touched?
How can emptiness feel so numb
and simultaneously sharper than a Japanese knife?

I am yearning for a soul like yours,
but one that stays rather than burns.
Maybe that's the lesson here.
The beauty of life is transience.
And even that will never stay.

Everyone will always leave.
Nothing is made to remain forever.
Not even these words.
Here for a moment,
a moment of passion, emotion,
a moment in motion

until it's gone.

It is the in-between that hurts the most.
The transition, the art
of letting go.
You are the artist
who creates your life.

Let the letting go be your muse.
As transformation fuelled by emotion
is your most powerful state of being.
Here's to feeling emotions so deep,
they cut through the thickest crust of denial.
Here's to the magic of metamorphosis,
to letting it all wash away with your tears.

Miss You

- After Gabrielle Calvocoressi

Miss you. Would like to take a walk with you
through fields of freedom and silent blue,
when our dreams were as big as the open sky
and our eyes shone brighter than the moon at night,
when possibilities were wider than the golden horizon,
when it felt so easy to be brave and brazen.

I search for you inside my heart
and feel the urge to fall apart.
What holds me together is knowing you're there,
in the wind of change that plays with my hair.
I hear the stars whisper: "You are not alone."
I sigh and trust you will guide me home.

A Silent Winter Night

Smoke plumes rising
from incense sticks
like soft, hairy feathers
lifting into the air
silently
The desire to touch it,
catch it, stroke it
Forever intangible
like you

The smell of orange zest
Juice drops on my plate
running down my fingers
turning sticky
Indulging in the taste
of winter sun-ripe citrus
Sweetness
in the air
A comforting scent
like yours

Lights dimmed
Candles flickering
Darkness
locked out behind glass

The mellow sound of jazz
playing in the background
Woollen blankets
A comfy winter night
Just like last year,
when you were still here.

The Last Time

We laugh until our bellies hurt
She pushes herself off the handrail
and turns her wheelchair into
a rickety box shaped race car
She's belting down the hallway
at the nursing home,
yodelling and squeaking.
Until she almost crashes
into another elderly lady.
All nurses and all residents
know her by her name,
Irene or Frau Degelmann
For me she's always been Oma,
the most joyful woman I know.
She loves a little shot
of eggnog before bed.
She says, at her age it's ok,
it doesn't matter anymore.
She also says that we should shoot
this Trump guy to the moon,
a one-way flight will suffice.
Listen to a wise woman's words.
Before I leave, she looks at me
"Do what brings you joy." And:
"Next time we will laugh again."

Listen to a wise woman's words.
Only that next time will have to be
in a different life.

The Last Cut

There is a paradox alive inside me.
It is the art of my mind, my heart's fantasy, my reality.
I am craving your love like soft chocolate fudge,
wishing the indulgence came without pain.
A love that leaves a scar before it even happens.
It cuts through my flesh to the depth of my bone,
leaving an eternal white trace on warm tanned skin.
But it leads nowhere.
Like permanent marker,
I try to rub and scrub and scratch
it off but it stays and stains.
And yet your mark on my heart is invisible.
Nobody can see the flame burning inside,
lighting up my heart like a warming hearth,
melting away my protective coat.
What is left is pure vulnerability.
For when the sword strikes
it is the point of no return,
the drama's climax, a tale's end. Please,
don't prove the fool wrong in a foolproof story.
It was never your sword,
not even your word.
It was my own thoughts, who have guided you in,
who opened the door to my heart's chamber.
You stepped inside with your shoes still on

to take over the space I had created for you.
As I stand in the light, I throw my own shade.
It had always been me who passed you the blade.
And I'm still hoping for you to leave it unused.

The Aftershave's Repercussion

There it is again
Your scent
lingering in my hair,
not letting me forget.

It was a brief hug,
that brought never-ending pain
filling the air
around me.

I believe they call it
the Axe effect.

Gravity

It is as if you were the sun
and I was one
of your planetarian girls.
Am I Venus, the lover?
Or Earth, the mother?
I am pulled
by the force of attraction
as if you were the centre
of gravity.
I am falling for you,
towards you,
but can never reach you,
eternally circling
around you.
Are you holding me on track
or keeping me trapped?
Are you sharing your light with me,
making me shine
or are you dimming mine?

If you are the moon,
I am the ocean.
You direct how I move,
let me rise and fall
And I am riding the tides

of my emotions.

You create the stars,
The world watches in awe.
Are they made with love
or for validation?
Are you the one
who is holding my world
together?
Or are you a black hole
swallowing me whole?
There is no escape.

Maybe you are just
another curve
in space and time.
Let's hope that Einstein
was right,
and all you are
is a little warp
in the galaxy
that is me.

Safe

I love the way you tease me
I can't wait for you to please me
You make me climb
heights I've never reached before
Sensations never met
like strangers on the street
A full body journey
into ecstasy
The cosmos inside me
bursts into
a billion sparks

Is this how stars are made?

The galaxy of nerves
awakens to expand
I'm breaking,
shaking and shivering
Paramount peaks of pivotal pleasure
collapsing, left quivering
left wanting more.

But you can't give me what I crave
- the feeling of being safe.

Something Smells Off

My milk bottle tipped over today
It reminded me of you.
It leaked over the fridge shelf,
a white wet puddle,
turning into sticky flakes,
a yellowish layer
that peels off emitting
a sourish legacy.
Just like you did
with your leaking lies.
The odour of decaying integrity
could have attracted maggots and flies.

The Right Person

Right person, wrong time?
How could the timing for the right one
ever be wrong?
Or is the time always right,
but maybe the person
is the one who isn't the one?
If timing doesn't align,
isn't that a sign?

If the person was right,
wouldn't you both re-align
the stars,
re-shuffle the cards
to be with each other?

Wouldn't you see them in a way
that made you stay
and so would they?

Cards on the table,
hearts on the table,
because the Queen of Hearts
doesn't use
timing as an excuse
to misuse

old patterns of fragility
to blame time's instability
for you to run away.
Love would have found a way.
But you rather run from responsibility
So, you don't have to respond
with your disability
to love
truly
deeply
to love yourself.

It is you who
will always understand yourself best,
but if you seek validation
from the rest
of the world,
you will get swirled up
in the mud
of masking, pretence,
performance and judgement
When all you needed was you.

You can only ever love someone
as much as
you love yourself.
The rest is co-dependence,

the rest is a house of cards,
the rest is made of empty words,
the rest is meant to break into shards.
What if the timing has always been right,
and the wrong person was you?

The Story

You liked my Instagram story
Next moment, the corners of my mouth
sneak up behind my ears.
I don't even notice it at first
until my heartbeat chimes in,
it skips and stumbles over its own childish
little feet. I roll my eyes at myself,
so far that I can almost see
the back of my frontal
cortex. Only that I'm not so sure
if my brain even exists.
How do you still have such
a big effect on me?
I would prefer you didn't
No, I would prefer
you. I would prefer you
had this effect and also truly
liked me. Instead of only
my story. What makes it worse
is that you always
like the ones that matter.
That's why I know
you like what makes me me.
You like me.
Just not quite enough
to make it love.

Excuse me, Sir

I am convinced you must be art
Something in the way you breathe
makes me gasp for air.
Your regalty is patent,
your appearance smart.

You've declared the streets your kingdom.
May my body be your home.
Your heartbeat plays the rhythm
of mystery and the unknown.
Let me dance to the song
that echoes in your bones.

I beg you, take me by your hand.
Show me your way,
your craft, your land.
But please, don't lose your modesty
so this won't end in tragedy.

Caught

Just when I thought
I was happier on my own,
when I felt still like the ocean
on a warm summer morning,
I caught you looking at me.

Loving You

Loving you feels like coming home
to a steaming mug of hot chocolate
    after a long winter hike.
I lean my forehead against
your firm chest
    underneath the soft fabric of your jumper.
Heat travels to my toes
and I keep my eyes closed
    so, I can pretend that time is standing still.

Am I allowed
to just feel
your presence?

I want to immerse myself in your aliveness,
in the deep soft freshness
    of blueish-green eyes,
the pleasant pain
of knowing
    that daylight always shifts.

Knowing you adore me, admire what I do
makes me want to serenade
    the magpies at the park.

It makes me beam
a foolish smile
      while brewing morning coffee.

I want you to explore
the landscape of my body,
      the mountains and the sea.
I want you to discover
      hidden corners of my mind.

Take my hand,
dive in with me
to find
      what nobody else gets to see.

The Thief Who Stole Your Eyes

Who is the thief
that stole your eyes
and replaced them with forest lakes?
So deep that I can't see
all the way down,
but the longing inside me loudly awakes.
I am due to drown
in you like ants
in a drop of morning dew.
I want to get drunk
on your mystery.
I want to be stitched
into your destiny.

My desires nest in your hair.
My hopes rest in the air
that you breathe.
With a sigh
you release
my despair
that was beating me up.
And I cry
as my heartbeat turns up
to interrupt
the peace.

I wear your kisses
like a necklace,
each one tracing my neck
seemingly reckless
along the seam of my collarless shirt
Where my collar bones hide
and wait
to stop you roam and guide
you home.

Your smile dismisses the soldiers
that have been guarding my heart.
Their endless duty is over.
Now they are dancing to the melody
that your hands left on my skin, singing:
        You are everything.

part 3: being in this world

or the union of beauty and pain that lies in the experience of being an individual in the complexity of this world

Pivot Point

What is good
and what is bad?
We all want to think
we are the good ones.
Nobody is.
All of us are.
We all justify our own actions
to prove to ourselves
that we are right.
   Oh, how righteous!
What if the gold lies in the middle?
What if the gold is staying open
to everyone's truth and peculiar perception?
Reality is absurdity's construct. Individuality.
None of it is absolute.
None of it - is definite.
   Oh, the audacity to call something true.
Please understand, you have no clue.
None of us do.
   All you can do is, don't lose your you.

Until the Sky Turns Blue Again

When he pressed the shutter release,
you could hear the cracking
echoing across the death-trenched land
as his soul shattered into pieces.

What his lens saw
had not been meant for his eyes to witness,
a burden too heavy to be carried
crushed his spirit
like a rock squishes ants.

The little girl, beaten by famine,
collapsed under the lurking gaze of vultures
an image his body would never forget.

There are places that seem
as if hope has left,
where the sky has given up
on trying to be blue,
where the earth is trenched
in the crimson of greed,
and the air is stenched
by the foulness of hatred.

Sometimes, the feeling of powerlessness

reaches its claws for my throat and chest,
paired with despair, pulling down on my feet.
I'm losing ground,
start to drown,
cannot breathe.

There are people risking their lives every day
to help those who are trapped between missile strikes.
Meanwhile, I am sitting at home,
my comfort feels sharply uncomfortable.

I wish I could save the world with my pen.
I would draw my own blood to use it as ink,
I would scratch the words into my skin
until it tears
unable to bear
the weight of the written.

But hurting myself won't stop others' pain.
Life is not easy for anyone.
One thing I can do
is share my presence with you.

A compliment, an honest smile
may not be the solution,
but sometimes it is all you need
to bring the light back home.

Grief destroys the strongest soul
if burdened by the shoulders
of one person alone.
So, I share my darkest thoughts with you
to let you know:
I feel it, too.

Born in a Burning House

Friends, my house is burning
and I can't stop the flames on my own.
The air is filled with smoke.
It bites my lungs, I can barely breathe, my eyes are watering.

This house has been my home, my place of nourishment.
This house is filled with beauty and all the people I love.
This house has given me everything
and never asked anything in return.
This house is my most treasured gift
but we have started to demolish it.

Friends, my house is burning
And I need your help.

I need you to stop buying clothes from Shein
and I need you to stop overeating meat.
I need you to start taking the train
and riding your bicycle more often.
I need you to vote for this planet
and consider your daily impact.
I need you to have shorter showers

and make better choices.

Friends, our house is burning
and I need us to do better.

I need us to think of singing birds
and imagine how life would be without them.
I need us to be grateful
for clean, running water and light.
I need us to stop taking things for granted
and pray that we will never have to starve.
I need us to understand that our privilege means
we are responsible.
I need us to finally take this seriously.

Yesterday I saw a bird collecting twigs to build a nest
in a tree that was cut down the day before.

Friends, Mother Earth is burning.

Hope

The fuel of life
The engine that keeps us moving
It pushes us out of bed in the morning
It drives us toward our goals

The hope to earn, to reach and achieve
The hope to succeed, meet love and be free
The hope for things to get a bit better
The hope that in the end it won't matter

The hope for the darkest place to get brighter
The hope for the deepest pain to get lighter

On days when you feel the burden of life
Hope will help you survive.
Those mornings you wake up feeling too blue
Hope will carry you through.

If there is no hope
there is no reason to live
there is only darkness
eternal gloom

But nothing in life is made to remain
The double-edged sword of impermanence

A soothing oath for things to end
Uniting hope and pain

Where there is hope, there will be life
Where there is life, there will be love

Love that coincides with joy
When you turn your gaze up high
And you spot a vibrant rainbow
in a dark and rain laden sky

Love that resides in the moment
when you have that first warm sip
of smooth barista-made coffee
the elixir touching your lip

Love that hides in the playful charm
when you're nudged by a dog's black nose
asking you with big amber eyes
to love them and keep them close

You can't give up on that, can you?
Try not to give up on love.
Please don't give up on life.
Never give up on hope.

Hope

- a searing force
yet gentle reminder
to live.

Girlband

- After Courtney Love

I'm going to find the meanest bitches and start a band.
I am going to celebrate other women for screaming their truth
into the polluted air of misogyny.
I am going to do everything
that anyone has ever told me I couldn't do.

I don't need to obey to your nonsense rules.
I don't need to thank you for paying back your debt.
I am not going to do what you sell as 'the best' for me
while you are trying to oppress me,
suppress my expression
so that no one can see
that you are holding me small
to make yourself look bigger.

Oh puppet, don't you know?

I have an army of women marching beside me.
We rebel and repel narcissistic halfwits
with a Master degree in manipulation theory.

You can't keep us down
because we are here to rise.

We help each other up,
dust off the denim jackets.
We wear grazed knees with pride and honour
like the lapel pins of war veterans.
We hold onto pens, mics and guitars
like patriarchs have been clutching the pitchforks.
And we will never cease singing
our songs of remembrance.

Like a Meteor

– After Audre Lorde

Have you ever been to Iceland and seen a geyser erupt?
Before it goes back to rest, seemingly peaceful
But the tranquillity deceives.
Below the surface the heat is rising, pressure emerging
The Earth is assembling her forces, her power, an
elemental army
Until she can no longer hold back.
She blows up and ejects her boiling tinctures
Hissing and fizzing with whistling anger
While you stand and stare,
Paralysed in awe of spectacular beauty
A threatening death trap if you stepped too close.

Have you ever stood at the abyss of a canyon
Gazing into the endless void
where the Earth has cracked open?
One moment in time after countless centuries
of silent slumber like Sleeping Beauty
Tectonic plates suddenly shifted,
tearing ancient rocks apart,
leaving a scar that you can't overlook
To remind generations of the Earth's mightiness.

Have you ever seen a crater and known

it took only one hit of celestial debris
to create a landscape that will last forever?

Don't take my silence for compliance.
Don't think yourself too safe while I'm watching.
For while I observe I gather my words
Like soldiers
ready to fight a battle against
Injustice, inequality and nature's depletion.
I only speak when I have something to say
And you better expect my pen to land heavy
I will make sure my words will stay
And leave a legacy that can't be forgotten
Like the deepest canyon, like a spitting volcano
"I'm going to go out like a fucking meteor"

Repercussion

Repercussion is an interesting word
morphologically at least
Its majority is percussion
The only difference is the prefix
As if there was a rhythm
that echoes back to you
Like a beat you've sent on a journey
but it boomerangs in a curve
and hits you in the face.
I think what we need
is less violent beating
and more groovy
dance beats.

Welcome Note

Welcome,
        please come closer,
                come in, take off
some layers
and make yourself un
                                    comfortable.

Let me show you my world,
So you might discover the infinit
-y
  of yours.

To your right, there is (cou-)
        rage hiding
        under the
        faded rose
        velvet couch
Lure her   out,
but choose your bait wisely.
If you can meet her with love, trust,
acceptance,
        she will respond with great
em   power   ment
But if you trick her, judge
and encage her,
        she will combust into a

m o n s t r o u s
                        inferno
and burn
   the house
                 down.

If you look straight ahead and lift
your gaze lightly,
you will spot my favourite place
a white window sill, a dark wooden frame
with an intricate stained
glass pattern on top
just like the one at the
Chelsea Hotel.
This is where the light likes to play,
to dance, to
          enchant, to be
foolish,   tricks
         to play
It is, where I sit to watch and listen,
to come back to presence,
stillness and ease.

Come closer, look deeper
Soften your gaze
and you will find joy
in simplicity –

the pleasure of being
>   here and now.

There is beauty in anything
your eyes will rest on,
clearly visible if you are willing to see
if you look with gratitude
    and curiosity.

I have put fresh towels on the bed for you.
The soothing scent of freshly washed linen
fills the air, settling in like cherry petals
sailing off the tree.
This is where you will dream
big.
Only if you know your dreams,
You can go and
>   follow
>   them.

There is a whole bag of adventure
in the kitchen cupboard,
right next to fun and play
Have as much as you would like
I recommend take plenty.
Some may have a side effect
of anxiety

Please, don't let that stop
    you.
Breathe, be brave
and know
It will be worth it.
        You are.

I hope your stay
        will move you.
Be aware that you may need
a whole new set of clothes
(beliefs)
as you outgrow the old ones.

And please call me, if you need
more questions.

I've Got Questions

I know that today is Sunday.
What I don't know is why
a week has
                        seven
        days.
Where did the artist
go/ sleep/ love
                        buy their materials from?

If plants grow in the earth,
what grows in the sky?
I remember having a conversation with
my friend
        a stranger
                  nobody
at the rainbow-coloured window overlooking
        the Eiffel Tour and the green
                violinist wearing a purple suit.

If anxiety doesn't have a colour, how
does it make me feel blue? How
does it make the world feel as if it had been dipped in
grey?

The Tenderest Shooting

She hit her head on the edge to fly
to spite herself,
to cut off her own kind of love.
Heaven
compared to being
where it's like a life raft.
The roots of those emotions - follow.
There is a skin removed.
He had always been an adoring parent.

Shoelaces

Shoelaces are tied
An outworn bequeathment of past blue Converse
His ritual hour of society
Eyes of a rock star,
only dull if you don't ask
the right questions twice
The big disappointment of commercialism
is woven into every inch
of his homemade habitualism
A religious ascetic
of the anguished loneliness
He used to be fun. He used to be wild.
Voices of his first ride
return to his face
as soot-blackened touches.
Another day pierces
after it sold the stars.
Minding her own business
had been the murder of his.

Pablo

Loose, rapid brushstrokes and dabs of colour
The clouds have been painted by Monet today.
I wonder what would happen
if they decided
to be printed by Andy Warhol.
Why do they never look like that?
Do clouds even like to do things for fun?
Would they feel pain if they had to be squeezed
into late Picasso's edgy cubes?
Pablo was a funny guy.
I think he only started to paint
rectangles because it was
too hard to imitate real life.
Have you seen his early works?
It's really not that good.
Nobody wants to say it out loud
but I am happy to be the one,
the onyx headed cat.
Nobody likes to do the things
they don't feel capable of.
Pablo disliked reality
and who could blame him for it?
So, he decided to make his own.
I want to be like Pablo.
I am.

Therapy

My favourite part about therapy
is when I can see tears in my therapist's eyes.
Not because she feels sorry for me,
not because she is hurting for me,
but because she has met the same pain as I.
It is those moments
when I feel less lonely.

The Polaroid

If I had no fear,
I would have kissed you
      on the night
you took the polaroid of us.
If I had no fear,
I would tell you
      here and now
that I want to see you again.
If I had no fear,
I would quit my job
      tomorrow
and become the world's greatest poet.
If I had no fear,
I would flirt with life
      every single day
and follow all my dreams.
If I had no fear,
I wouldn't wait
      until it is too late
to do it all.
If I had no fear,
I wouldn't stay silent
      ever again
but let my heart speak the truth.
      Always.

(Bio)Logic

If I was too much,
then why are there so many
other people in this world?

Sonic Love Affair

Chaotic chatter fills the space
like rain drops flirting with the air
like strong and turbulent ocean moans
Baristas yelling coffee orders
beating mellow background tunes
from someone's sunny balcony
A motorbike rumbles past
car tires knocking cobblestones,
Cyclists click clack to grab cappuccinos
Spoons hitting glasses while coffee is stirred
Knives cling on plates when smashed avo is served
Bread crunches, someone munches
The ocean breeze hums in my ear
A cheeky bird chirps while another one sings
I sit in silence, listening deeply.
Sound waves washing over me,
envelop me in a murmuring blanket
There's comfort in the indistinct.
Until the shrill squeak of a chair
rips me out
of my sonic love affair.

Leaving

Autumn has arrived
and it is time to let go
Two seasons I have served with pleasure
the tree, the mother, our family
I've opened myself to fully receive
the light and warmth of nourishing sun beams
I've collected raindrops to quench her thirst.
I've guided the waters to Mother Tree's roots.
I've shared my energy
with my community,
provided shelter to insects and birds.
The remuneration was pure joy.
I hold myself with pride.
I know about my uniqueness.
Yet, I'm aware that I alone
can't keep the tree alive.
She needs us all, in unity.
Each of us is treasured.
But now it is time
to finally rest.
I shall let go.
I let myself fall
with and into trust.
For as I turn brown
I become the earth

that nourishes my descendants.
And so, I close this circle of life.
Let's see what the next season will bring.

The Scent of Pines

A soft, gentle breeze
is playing with my hair
brushing against my neck
A furtive touch of soothing cool air
the tender-hearted wind
caressing my skin.

I close my eyes and I breathe in.
I smell the seductively charming scent
of freshly baked bread and sun-kissed pines.
Red wine and geraniums
are tantalising my senses.

I taste the alluring invitation
to drift away and forget it all,
to leave the heavily laden realm
of rapidly turning wheels.

An ephemeral moment of sacred stillness,
a sojourn in serenity

in a world of constant change.

Question

When can I stop to work full time?
Why am I so tired?
How am I meant to do it all?
Why can't others see me?
Am I loved?
Do I have to?
What is next?
What do I really want?
Can I please have more freedom?
How do I meet more good people?
Why do we have to work so much?
Why is there so much sadness?
Why is there war in the world?
Where is all the love?

What if I did all the things I'm scared of?
What if I wasn't scared?
What if I did all the things I want to do?
What if I said all the things I want to say?
What if I really listened to my heart?

Clouds

What if it isn't about
finding the sun on a cloudy day?
What if it is about trusting
that she's always here anyway?
What if it is about
finding poetry in the clouds?

Message from the Author and Acknowledgement

Hey, thanks for buying my book. It really means a lot. I have put myself on the vulnerability line with this, the space where cringe and authenticity overlap. In the process of creating this book I have successfully ignored the fact that published word stays and that it is accessible to whoever wants to read it. On top of that, my name is on the cover. There is no way to get out of this now, other than changing my name.

And yet, for some reason, I like being the odd one who says the things that make everyone feel a bit awkward, even though everyone has been secretly thinking the same anyway.

I am hoping that this book makes you feel seen, understood and maybe a little bit less lonely out there. Knowing that there are other people who share similar experiences and emotions to ours, can feel very soothing and peaceful. This is the experience of 'sonder' – the profound realisation that every random person out there has "a life as vivid and complex as your own". Everyone has a story, or better, uncountable stories.

I would like to acknowledge that this book has been mainly written on Whadjuk Noongar Boodja. The Traditional Owners of this land, the Noongar people are deeply connected to their community, family and the land. They teach us that we cannot thrive without community.

I can say that I would have never been able to write this book without my community. Please lt me take the chance and say thank you to a few of them in particular.

Cass – You welcomed me into your beautiful, safe poetry bubble, you saw me, you encouraged me and held me. Thank you. There is no way I would have ever considered writing and publishing poetry like this without you. I am excited for everything that is yet to come.

Chelsie Diane – You keep blowing my mind pretty much every day. Discovering your classes was the catapult I needed to make things happen last year. What I cherish the most about you is how deeply and truly you love every single woman in your community. You are the queen of 'no bullshit', only love and a tonne of sass.

Jae – Thank you for letting me follow you like a puppy dog. Thank you for helping me grow, for seeing me, for inspiring me. In times I don't know what to do, I often ask myself: "What would Jae do?" And then I go and slay. Thank you for being so openly vulnerable and authentic – There is nothing more courageous in this world.

Britt – You were the best therapist I've ever had. You made a difference. I will never forget that.

Lisa, Silke, Katrin – I love you. You have been there for me throughout almost my whole life, even after moving to the other end of the world. The 'Sex and the City' friendship every woman dreams of, but in real life.

Bree, Jae, Livia, Candice & Amanda – Thank you for taking the time to proof read my poetry and providing feedback. I deeply appreciate it. Hitting the submission button felt safer because of all of you.

Mama & Papa – You have done an amazing job raising me and I will be forever grateful for your ongoing support with everything. Thank you for letting me dream big and helping me making my dreams come true, no matter how crazy those dreams have been.

Two things I know for certain are that we are all going to die and that pain is inevitable. So, what do you have to lose? Could you please all go out there, be the main character of your life and make your dreams come true? Cheers.

www.ingramcontent.com/pod-product-compliance
Lightning Source LLC
Chambersburg PA
CBHW022116090426
42743CB00008B/868